AF255219

Pearls

Pearls

God's Inspired Word in Haiku

Karen DiNobile

RESOURCE *Publications* · Eugene, Oregon

PEARLS
God's Inspired Word in Haiku

Resource Publications
An Imprint of Wipf and Stock Publishers
199 W. 8th Ave., Suite 3
Eugene, OR 97401

www.wipfandstock.com

PAPERBACK ISBN: 978-1-6667-6793-3
HARDCOVER ISBN: 978-1-6667-6794-0
EBOOK ISBN: 978-1-6667-6795-7

VERSION NUMBER 013123

Dedicated To our awesome God, Father, Son and Holy Spirit, and to my wonderful, supportive family with which He has blessed me!

Every good thing given and every perfect gift is from above, coming down from the Father of lights, with whom there is no variation or shifting shadow (James 1:17)

Preface

It wasn't until I was in my fifties that I started reading the Bible. I had started watching TV preachers and teachers, intrigued that the Bible contained so much information about how to live life according to God's will. I purchased my very first study Bible, which explained Scripture and how to apply it to your life. I never realized how rich, rewarding and enjoyable studying Scripture could be! The one I first purchased was the amplified version. After that I bought several other versions, such as the NIV, and read, and continue to read, each chapter in their different versions.

Scripture contains so many little "gems," or pearls of great price! Matthew 13:45–46, states that "Again, the kingdom of heaven is like a merchant seeking fine pearls, and upon finding one pearl of great value he went and sold all that he had and bought it." Jesus is *the* Pearl of Great Price! He sacrificed His life to purchase us, and taught us, through the Gospels, that He is the Way, the Truth, and the Life. (John 14:6) He can be found by those who diligently seek Him, and when you find this Pearl of Great Price, you have found eternal life!

We are all unique, and most likely will have different pearls of great price. For instance, one pearl may be John

3:16, "For God so loved the world that He gave His only begotten Son, that whoever believes in Him shall not perish but have eternal life." Or Jeremiah 29:11, "For I know the plans that I have for you," declares the Lord, "plans for welfare and not for calamity to give you a future and a hope." Or perhaps the beloved Psalm 23, which begins, "The Lord is my Shepherd, I shall not want…" Or maybe the wisdom of Proverbs 16:3: Commit your works to the Lord and your plans will be established." The whole Bible is a pearl of great price!!

I have written but a few examples, in haiku form, of how Scripture can impact your life! Read each one, then the referring Scripture, and comments about how it can be applied to your life. Every human emotion, every problem, is covered in the Bible, God's handbook for living.

Get a study Bible, see what pearls you can find of your own. Discover Jesus in every book of the Bible, in the Old Testament prophecies, to the New Testament Gospels and epistles. The Bible contains many of the promises of God, but you cannot claim them if you don't know them, and you can't know them unless you read the Bible!

My hope for you in writing this upbeat, light-hearted book about Scripture is to encourage you, uplift you, cause you to pause and see how much more of an abundant life you can have from reading and applying the principles and teachings in the Bible to your own life. May you find the Pearl of Great Value, and many other pearls of your own. It is an exciting journey!

God bless!

Abbreviations of Scripture

OLD TESTAMENT

Gen	Genesis
Josh	Joshua
1–2 Chr	Chronicals
Job	Job
Ps (pl. Pss)	Psalm
Eccl	Ecclesiastes
Isa	Isaiah
Jer	Jeremiah
Ezek	Ezekiel
Mic	Micah

NEW TESTAMENT

Matt	Matthew
Mark	Mark
John	John
Acts	Acts
Rom	Romans
1–2 Cor	Corinthians
Eph	Ephesians
Phil	Philippians

Col	Colossians
1–2 Thess	Thessalonians
Titus	Titus
Jas	James
1–2 Peter	Peter
1–2-3 John	John

road trip through my soul
not knowing the way but
knowing the Waymaker

John 14:6

"I am the way, the truth and the life; no one comes to the Father but through me."

Jesus said that He IS the way, the truth, and the life. As long as we follow His way, we will never be lost, not in mind, spirit or body. He is, after all, the Way to the Father, to salvation, to our forever home.

third stage of life
Lord, help me to understand
the cycle of me

Prov 3:5–6

Trust in the Lord with all your heart and do not lean on your own understanding. In all your ways acknowledge Him and He will make your paths straight.

God has an individual plan for each one of us in every stage of our life. If we surrender our lives to Him, and ask Him to guide us, He will. You must believe that it is the best possible plan. He loves you and wants you to bear fruit for your joy and to better serve His people and bring glory to Him.

diagnosis day
in my pocket
a packet of mustard seed

Matt 17:20

"If you have faith the size of a mustard seed, you will say to this mountain, 'Move from here to there,' and nothing will be impossible to you."

Jesus said, "If you have faith the size of a mustard seed ..." The mustard seed is the smallest of all seeds; we don't have to start out with great faith—that grows with studying scripture, with prayer, with remembering past times that God has indeed answered those prayers. Start small; it's ok; start with a mustard seed of faith!

feather in the wind
His still small voice
whispers to my soul

Isa 30:21

Your ears will hear a word behind you, "This is the way, walk in it," whenever you turn to the right or to the left.

In the silence of our souls, God speaks to us. It is a gentle calling, maybe a prompting, and it is soft, reassuring and comforting to your soul. He never forces but guides us, through His Holy Spirit, in the way we should go, quietly, softly…like a feather.

harshness of winter
promise of spring
forgiveness

Eph 4:31–32

"Let all bitterness and wrath and anger and clamor and slander be put away from you, along with all malice. Be kind to one another, tender-hearted, forgiving each other, just as God in Christ also has forgiven you."

Bitterness and anger cause us to be harsh, unforgiving. However, as God has forgiven us, we must also forgive each other, not only for the other person but for ourselves. If we don't forgive, neither will our heavenly father forgive us our sins. God is the avenger of all unfairness done to you. Let go, let God!

comfortably clothed for winter sparrows

Matt 6:26

"Look at the birds of the air, that they do not sow, nor reap nor gather into barns, and yet your heavenly Father feeds them. Are you not worth much more than they?"

God not only feeds the birds but supplies a warm coat for winter months! God is our source, not our bank account or paycheck; he is responsible for our needs and will supply them richly, if we do our part and if we only believe, and honor Him, praise Him and give Him thanks for everything!

sign on the door of my soul:
closed for renovations
Holy Spirit at work

Titus 3:4–7

Jesus saved us, not on the basis of deeds which we have done in righteousness but according to His mercy, by the washing of regeneration and renewing by the Holy Spirit.

One of the functions of the Holy Spirit is to help us to let go of our former, sinful ways, and be renewed and guided by the work of the Holy Spirit, to be regenerated as it were, to be made new in body, mind and spirit, to be made into the likeness of Christ. Romans 12:2 exhorts us to " … not be conformed to this world, but transformed by the renewing of your mind."

before the birds
I awaken the dawn
in prayer and praise

Ps 57:8–9

Awake, my glory! Awake harp and lyre! I will awaken the dawn. I will give thanks to You, O Lord, among the peoples; I will sing praises to You among the nations.

Do you awaken the dawn with praise and thanksgiving to almighty God, confident that his love and protection will be with you throughout the day? Many people believe the best time to meditate and pray is in the silence before the family gets up, before the busyness of the day, but praise and thanksgiving are appropriate any time of the day!

conductor
of the music in my soul
Yahweh

Ps 108:1,3

My heart is steadfast, O God; I will sing, I will sing praises, even with my soul. I will give thanks to you, O Lord, among the peoples, and I will sing praises to You among the nations.

Sing and make music to our God, who is the conductor of the symphony in your life! We can praise Him with song, music, in our places of worship, in our homes, in our very being. God is awesome! Praise be to God!

an eagle angles into
a taste of sky
high hopes

Jer 29:11

"For I know the plans that I have for you, declares the Lord, "plans for welfare and not for calamity to give you a future and a hope."

Do you believe that God keeps his promises, that He answers prayers, or are you just hoping it's true? God's plans for us are to give us hope, to prosper, to always come up higher in our faith, in our walk with Him. As the psalmist said in Psalm 130:5, "I wait for the LORD, my whole being waits, and in His word I put my hope."

golden sunrises silver sunsets
riches beyond measure
I am blessed

Ps 113:3

From the rising of the sun to its setting the name of the
Lord is to be praised.

Do you ever take getting up and going to bed for granted?
Do you take time to marvel at the sunrise and sunset?
These are awesome gifts God gives us to enjoy and con-
template, riches beyond measure. Take time tonight, to-
morrow morning to see God's incredible works and praise
Him.

the glory of the heavens
reflected in the waters
my soul with my God

2 Cor 3:18

But we all, with unveiled face, beholding as in a mirror the glory of the Lord, are being transformed into the same image from glory to glory, just as from the Lord, the Spirit.

Does your soul reflect the glory of God, as does creation? Look into a lake or pool, the reflection of the sky, the trees, even an eagle flying over it. You are God's creation, being transformed from glory to glory! Let us reflect His glory!

soft spring rain
I lift my face in praise
my forehead is anointed

Job 5:10

He gives rain on the earth and sends water on the fields.

Soft spring rain. Forget the umbrella! Lift up your face to the skies, feel the anointing of gentle rain and praise God who created it!

my "yes" to follow Him
my pearl
of great price

Matt 13:45–46

Again, the kingdom of heaven is like a merchant seeking fine pearls, and upon finding one pearl of great value, he went and sold all that he had and bought it.

Matt 9:9

As Jesus went on from there, He saw a man called Matthew, sitting in the tax collector's booth; and He said to him, "Follow Me!" And he got up and followed Him.

What do you treasure most? What is your "pearl of great price?" Is it your decision to follow Jesus, the joy of your salvation? Matthew, a tax collector, left everything to follow Jesus and received blessings beyond measure, becoming one of Jesus' 12 apostles. Nothing can compare to following Him and receiving His love, redemption and forgiveness of sins, the price He paid for us at the cross. We are His pearl of great price!

the flower bends to the sun
so my heart yields
to Him

Mic 6:8

He has told you, "O man, what is good; and what does the Lord require of you but to do justice, to love kindness and walk humbly with your God?"

The flower bends to the sun as it grows. When we yield ourselves to God, submit to His most perfect plan for our lives, we too will grow in the likeness of His Son, Jesus and receive the blessing of the Almighty. Yield!

stay-at-home mom
in her element
in His calling

Psalm 139:16

Your eyes have seen my unformed substance; and in Your book were written the days that were ordained for me when as yet there was not one of them.

God has a plan for your life that was established before you were born! If you enjoy and get satisfaction from what you are doing, whether a stay-at-home mom or a person in the outside work field, you are in God's will! He gives you the strength, the desire to do what you are doing. If you are not sure of God's will for your life, just ask Him! He will most assuredly answer that prayer: "Lord, what would You have me do with my life?"

grace
the gravitational pull
of God's love

Eph 1:7

In Him we have redemption through His blood, the forgiveness of our trespasses, according to the riches of His grace.

Eph. 2:8–9

For by grace you have been saved through faith; and that not of yourselves, it is the gift of God; not as a result of works so that no one may boast.

Grace is God's unmerited favor, God's love in action in our lives. He gently pulls us to himself if only we yield! It is a choice. We are saved by grace, live by grace, and forgiven of our sins by grace through belief in his son, Jesus.

night canvas
God's handiwork
in each star

Ps 147:4

He counts the number of stars; He gives names to all of
them.

How awesome is our God! Look at the stars and try to
contemplate that each one was given a name by our al-
mighty God! The beauty of stars, truly a blessing and a
gift for us to enjoy!

wilderness
in its midst a deep well
to draw from faith to faith

Rom 1:17

For in it (the gospel) the righteousness of God is revealed from faith to faith; as it is written, "But the righteous man shall live by faith."

Whatever wilderness you may be experiencing now, be it sickness, unemployment, anxiety, faith in God's promises will keep you going, for it is said, the righteousness of God will lead you from faith to faith. He will deliver you from the wilderness or take you through it. Believe it. By faith!

being a poet
the one in the family
who flies out of formation

Rom 12:6

Since we have gifts that differ according to the grace given to us, each of us is to exercise them accordingly…

God has given different gifts and talents to each one of us. If no one understands your gift, take heart-He does! We are all unique, with different God-given talents and abilities. Let's celebrate each other's gifts and thank God for our own. Be bold! Dare to fly out of formation!

do not give up little bird
you're only one flight
from home

2 Chr 15:7

"But you, be strong and do not lose courage, for there is reward for your work."

You may never know how close you have come to your destination, to your goal, if you give up. You may send out 50 resumes and not get a response, but the 51st might be the one that gets the response. God gives strength to the weary, so when you think you can't go on, ask God for help to go on. You may never know how close you have come to your destination, to your goal, if you give up.

last leaf dangles
falls away
you always think you have more time

Eccl 3:2

A time to give birth and a time to die; a time to plant and a time to uproot what is planted.

This verse states that there is a time for birth and death. No one knows when they will go home to be with the Lord. We must therefore make the most of each day, of all that God has given us. Never forget to say I love you, make time to spend with your family, with God in prayer and meditation. Laugh more! Dance! You always think you have more time with that special someone, but you never know.

preschool
teaching children
the colors of love

Ps 127:3

Behold, children are a gift of the Lord, the fruit of the womb is a reward.

Love is a verb. You teach kids about love by loving them, in the home, in the classroom. Color their world with love, by example in what you do, how you act, what you say. They will then learn to love others. Children are a gift from the Lord.

interior decorator
getting rid of the clutter
in my soul

1 John 1:9

If we confess our sins, He is faithful and righteous to forgive us our sins and to cleanse us from all unrighteousness.

Sometimes we carry around a weight in our hearts and soul and don't know why. What clutters a soul? Unconfessed sin, definitely. Or not doing something God asked us to do but didn't do which can make us feel guilty. The verse above states that if we confess our sins God will forgive us of all our sins. His grace and forgiveness—how uplifting. He is the best de-clutterer you can ever get! And what does He ask in return? Faith! For without faith, it is impossible to please God (Hebrews 11:6).

unexpected guests
on my front porch
cherry blossoms

Jas 1:17

Every good thing given and every perfect gift is from above, coming down from the Father of lights, with whom there is no variation or shifting shadows.

God's gifts can bless you when you don't even expect it! Maybe you're in a hurry, rushing to work or an appointment, you open the front door and there is a "good and perfect gift from above," the beauty of cherry blossoms, causing you to pause and welcome your unexpected guests! How awesome God is!

easier now
to scatter seed
social media

Mark 16:15

And he said to them, "Go into all the world and preach the gospel to all creation."

Social media: So many ways to communicate today! Facebook, Twitter, Instagram, email, texting…how easy it is now to scatter the seed of God's word to the world! We have a unique opportunity to evangelize that wasn't available 20 years ago. The joy that fills your heart from knowing God, from knowing you are saved with belief in Jesus, share it with others. How can you not!!

eternity
the shelf life
of His grace

2 Cor 9:8

And God is able to make all grace abound to you, so that always having all sufficiency in everything, you may have an abundance for every good deed.

God's grace is God's favor poured out in abundance. Prayer activates faith which activates God's grace. Pray!

finding a penny
I am reminded of
God's awesome provision

Phil 4:19

My God will supply all your needs according to His riches in glory in Christ Jesus.

Every time I find a penny or any coin I pick it up. It reminds me of God's awesome provision for every area of life. He is our Source for, as Philippians above states, ALL our needs. How about you? Next time you find a coin, go ahead, pick it up and joyfully affirm the provision of our mighty God!

I catch a money bug
    then
        let it go

Matt 6:24

No one can serve two masters, for either he will hate the one and love the other, or he will be devoted to one and despise the other. You cannot serve God and wealth.

Josh 24:15

Choose this day whom you will serve…but as for me and my house, we will serve the Lord.

Jesus stated, "You can't serve God and mammon (money). Which god do you serve? The god of money? Power? Title? Prestige? All of these things are temporary. Loving money leads to greed, selfishness, jealousy. As 1 Timothy 6:10 states, "For the love of money is a root of all sorts of evil … " But the God of the universe, who made heaven and earth and everything on and in it, this our God, is eternal, who gives us His love, grace, mercy, forgiveness joy and peace without measure, who gives us everything we need. So which God or gods do you serve?

stars
competing for brightness
the Emmys of space

1 Cor 12:5–6

Now there are varieties of gifts, but the same Spirit. And there are varieties of ministries, and the same Lord. There are varieties of effects but the same God who works all things in all persons.

One star shines brighter than another—or does it? We are all given special gifts and talents, and even then, in differing degrees. We don't have to compete for an Emmy because we all shine in the eyes of God, who gives us perfect gifts according to His most perfect will.

two more decades
of the rosary before him
truck driver

Modern Haiku Volume 48.3 Autumn 2017

Eph 6:18

With all prayer and petition pray at all times in the Spirit, and with this in view, be on the alert with all perseverance and petition for all the saints.

There are many long roads in life. What you choose to do with them can help determine the outcome. Praying and meditating on the rosary, or saying favorite prayers, will help stay your mind and give you peace, for the long haul, even if just for the "short haul."

half moon
his pain
after my surgery
Frogpond Volume 38 number 1

Ps 119:76

O may Your lovingkindness comfort me according to
Your word to Your servant.

When someone we love is hurting, we suffer along with
that person, differently but in pain for what they are going
through. Thank God we have a Comforter who comforts
us so we can comfort others! (2 Corinthians 1:4) It is not
easy, but he gives us the comfort and strength to see our
loved one through the pain and comforts our loved one
and us as well.

farmer's hand to plow
the communion of
heart and soul

Matt 22:37

You shall love the Lord your God with all your heart, and with all your soul, and with all your mind.

The Bible commands that we love God with our whole heart, mind and soul. When we do, we have the ultimate communion of heart and soul. It's like the farmer who puts his heart into his work, plowing, to develop a crop. When we love God with all we've got, that's when we are united heart and soul.

top notch surgeon
for open heart surgery
God

Ezek 36:26

I will give you a new heart and put a new spirit in you; I will remove from you your heart of stone and give you a heart of flesh.

We can get a hardened heart from bitterness, resentment or refusal to forgive. We can put up a wall of indifference to events and people in the world around us. We need to guard against these harmful things and pray to God to help soften our hearts and be more compassionate and caring. He will!

coming to the end of self
beginning the journey
to Him

Isa 43:18–19

Thus says the Lord, "Do not call to mind the former things, or ponder things of the past. Behold, I will do something new. Now it will spring forth. Will you not be aware of it? I will even make a roadway in the wilderness, rivers in the desert."

When you have exhausted all means of taking care of yourself and your problems, and don't know what to do or who to turn to, that's when you turn your life over to God. He will bring about peace, comfort, restoration and renewed hope. No matter what your wilderness or where you've been, He is the answer, and will make a new road for you out of the wilderness! It is of God and He will direct your steps on the journey!

a thousand tea bags
would not be enough
wild mint
Modern Haiku Volume 52.1 Winter-Spring 2021

2 Cor 9:8

And God is able to make all grace abound to you, so that always having all sufficiency in everything, you may have an abundance for every good deed.

Wild mint! No matter how much you pick, there's always more! Kind of like God's grace—you can never use it up. God's grace is God's favor, and He longs to show favor to you. Just ask him!

the tide comes in goes out
leaves its wave prints on the shore
endlessly

I Cor 15:58

Therefore, my beloved brethren, be steadfast, immovable, always abounding in the work of the Lord, knowing that your toil is not in vain in the Lord.

The tide comes in, goes out; our problems, challenges and trials come and go throughout our lives. Endlessly. But our God remains steadfast and constant and will be with us in all our ups and downs, ins and outs. Endlessly!

giving retirement
all that you've got
somewhere a train whistle

Ps 92:14

They (the righteous) will still yield fruit in old age; they shall be full of sap and very green.

Retirement is not the ending of dreams or accomplishment, but just another station of life. But it is a choice: to sit back and take it easy, or listen to that whistle inside that calls you to new and as yet unknown, adventures! Go for it! God will be with you at every station!

positive test
they add another branch
to their family tree

Ps 128:3,4

Your wife shall be like a fruitful vine within your house, your children like olive plants around your table. Behold, for thus shall the man be blessed who fears the Lord.

The above Psalm states that the one who fears (reverently) the Lord will have children like olive shoots around their table. Having children can mean natural, adopted, those you love and care for like your own. Children are a blessing and gift from the Lord, as parents, grandparents, caretakers and all who love children will affirm! God bless our children!

enjoying roadside flowers
the incessant beep of those
behind me

Ps 96:12

Let the field exult, and all that is in it…

Maybe while we are waiting for a light to change, or slowed down by traffic, we see something of beauty on the side of the road and it delights us and we take time to take it in. However, those in back of us do not take notice or don't care. They are in a hurry and want you to be too! Thank God for His creations and making you aware of them; take your joy with you and move on!

in the midst of
that sterile environment
a gloved hand speaks

2 Cor 1:3–4

Blessed be the God and Father of our Lord Jesus Christ, the Father of mercies and God of all comfort, who comforts us in all our affliction so that we will be able to comfort those who are in any affliction with comfort with which we ourselves are comforted by God.

During the pandemic, so many people died or were seriously ill. Family members were not allowed in hospitals but there were front line workers, nurses, doctors who, because of their great compassion, held a dying person's hand, or comforted a scared patient, going above and beyond their duties, heroes in every way, in compassion and love. Sometimes a gloved hand speaks more than words.

depression
my soul in shadows
I turn towards the Son

Matt 11:28

"Come to me all you who are weary and heavy laden and I will give you rest."

Jesus is the Light of the world (John 8:12); He can lift your soul from the dark pit of depression that we sometimes are in, and transfer you to his Light. As you let his Light wash over you, you will feel your depression lift. Turn to the Son!

I find a bug upside down
and turn him
right side up

Gen 1:21

God created the great sea monsters and every living creature that moves…and God saw that it was good.

God created every living creature that moves and we should treat Nature with compassion when we see one of those creatures in distress, be it an animal being abused—or a bug that can't right itself!

the last leaf leaves
the oak without notice
his brief obituary

Col 3:23

Whatever you do, do your work heartily as for the Lord, knowing that from the Lord you will receive the reward of the inheritance. It is the Lord Christ whom you serve.

Most people will not attain fame or fortune or get to influence thousands of others. But we are important to God, who has equipped each of us with different gifts and talents and purpose in life. And we do make a difference to our family, friends, co-workers, all with whom we come in contact. The only thing that matters is what matters to God, so at our entrance into His holy, joyful kingdom, He can say, "Well done, good and faithful servant." That is our legacy, that we loved God, obeyed Him and fulfilled His purpose in our life.

God
has a sense of humor
mothers-in-law!

Matt 5:9

Blessed are the peacemakers for they shall be called sons of God.

Eph 4:2

…with all humility and gentleness, with patience, showing tolerance for one another in love.

Some people have a wonderful mother-in-law, while others have a person that is hard to love, or a challenge to get along with! However, sometimes God will place those who we see as unlovable, in our life to act as sandpaper, to teach us, so He can smooth our rough edges, prepare us for the awesome plan he has for us. Yes, it is a challenge of patience, tolerance, but oh so worth it! Offer up your challenge to Him, and ask Him to work out any negative traits in you. You may just as well be a challenge to that mother-in-law!

working from home
how can I think, bird,
with you singing? Sing, bird!

Ps 118:24

This is the day the Lord has made; let us rejoice and be glad it.

Still working from home? Many companies have decided to postpone returning or allow some employees to work from home permanently. Working from home can be both rewarding and stressful. Where is the joy? Listen! Is that a song bird? Would you hear that bird if you were at the office? Perhaps he is there to cheer you up! Each day has its problems and joy! Find the joy, pray for strength and guidance to get through. "God is our refuge and our strength…" (Psalm 46:1)

April eve
where do these breezes go
after they refresh the soul?

Jer 31:25

"For I satisfy the weary ones and refresh everyone who languishes," says the Lord of hosts.

We all need times of refreshing. Being in nature is one of the best ways to refresh your mind, your body, your soul. Take a walk, go out on your porch or just open a window and feel the fresh breeze of renewal. Breathe it in, then let it go …

nature
God's living Bible

Psalm 96:11

Let the heavens be glad, and let the earth rejoice; let the
sea roar and all it contains.

The Bible is God's inspired Word; nature is God's physi-
cal Bible, abounding in sights and sounds, talking to us,
teaching us, informing us of His greatness! Spend a part of
every day outside, experience nature in sight and sound.
He created nature for us. Dance with the wind! Laugh at
the clouds! Turn your face up to the gentle rain! God is
speaking, listen to Him!

church graveyard
soft snow covers
the gravestone dates

John 3:16

For God so loved the world, that He gave His only begotten Son, that whoever believes in Him shall not perish, but have eternal life.

Probably the most famous Bible verse in the New Testament, it states that whoever believes in Jesus will not die but have eternal life. And 2 Corinthians 5:8 states that when absent from the body you are present with the Lord. Therefore, the dates on the gravestone represent the birth and earthly date of departure, for their souls are with the Lord. Forever! How reassuring!

morning warbler
freer now than I was
in quarantine

1 Thess 5:18

Rejoice always; pray without ceasing; in everything give thanks, for this is God's will for you in Christ Jesus.

What freedoms did you miss most during the pandemic? Time with family and friends? Going to work at the office or place of employment? Going to school? Sports? Gym? Not wearing a face mask? It's amazing what we take for granted and don't appreciate until they are taken away! I told my family to write down what they missed most, and when the pandemic was over, to appreciate them even more! How about you?

each blink of a firefly
lasts for but a moment
and yet…

Matt 5:16

Jesus said, "Let your light shine before men in such a way that they may see your good works, and glorify your Father who is in heaven."

Acts of light can last but for a moment, but each one has an impact on those you shine it on: A smile, a hug, a wave, saying "I love you." Go ahead, let your moments of light shine before others, it's those "good works" that others will remember! It's God working through you, and He gets the glory!

meditation garden
no words just the sigh
of … butterflies?

Isa 63:3

The steadfast of mind You will keep in perfect peace because he trusts in You.

When we meditate and are in the presence of God, no words, no prayers are necessary. We enjoy a feeling of peace, of contentment of knowing He is with us. Sometimes we may unknowingly sigh and startle ourselves and wonder where did that come from? We ask ourselves, "Do butterflies sigh?" Or is it the release of that joy and peace that must express itself? And we know then that all is well with our soul!

excluded from the club
I thought I knew
who I was

2 Cor 5:17

Therefore if anyone is in Christ, he is a new creature; the old things passed away; behold, new things have come.

What "club" have you been excluded from? The club that celebrates "me?" That one that is obsessed with money or title or power? When you accept Jesus as Lord and Savior, you belong to Him, and are in the world but no longer of the world. God has a calling on your life! You were never actually a member of that club, you were looking for more, something deeper. Now you know who you truly are—a new creation in Christ and are free from any club "rules" such as gaining status or power or any of those listed above! You are free, free, free!

winter spring always

Isa 40:4

Let every valley be lifted up, and every mountain and hill be made low; and let the rough ground become a plain, and the rugged terrain a broad valley.

Every valley experience we have, our winters, our deserts, are always followed by mountain top experiences, our springs. Always. You must remember that neither lasts forever, for there will always be winters and springs in your life. Know that God is with you through it all. Valley experiences are a time to pray. Mountain top experiences, a time to praise!

morning night
night morning
when God when?

2 Pet 3:8

But do not let this one fact escape your notice, beloved, that with the Lord one day is like a thousand years, and a thousand years like one day.

Eccl 3:1

There is an appointed time for everything. And there is a time for every event under heaven.

God's timing is not our timing. He is usually not early, but never late, according to His most perfect timing. Do not be anxious that your prayer, your petition has not been answered yet. God's timing is always perfect. Perhaps He is getting someone or something ready that you are not aware of, or it's just not the right time for it to be granted; He may be teaching you patience! Do not worry or think he has not heard your petition. He has and he will answer—in his perfect timing!

grass and crabgrass
all the same
to the sun

Acts 10:34

Peter said, "I most certainly understand now that God is not one to show partiality."

The same sun that shines on grass shines on crabgrass and weeds. Just so, whoever believes in the Son of God is welcome in His kingdom. For, "… if you confess with your mouth Jesus as Lord, and believe in your heart that God raised Him from the dead, you will be saved." (Romans 10:9)

Seasons of Joy

summer hammock me and my cat

colors of fall my calico cat

cozy cat
safe from storms and cold
me and my indoor cat

new growth new buds new life
me and my spring cat-
and kittens!